*sparknotes

TOO LONG; DIDN'T READ

TL;DR
LITERATURE

This 2022 edition printed for SparkNotes, LLC, by Sterling Publishing Co., Inc.

ISBN 978-1-4114-8072-8
ISBN 978-1-4114-8073-5 (e-book)

For information about custom editions, special sales, and premium purchases,
please contact specialsales@unionsquareandco.com.

Printed in Malaysia

2 4 6 8 10 9 7 5 3 1

sparknotes.com
unionsquareandco.com

Cover and interior design by Gina Bonanno
Endpapers by Gina Bonanno
Illustrations: MUTI *c/o* Folio Art Limited

Image credits: **Shutterstock.com:** 67

*sparknotes

TOO LONG; DIDN'T READ

TL;DR

LITERATURE

Dynamically illustrated plot and character
summaries for 13 modern classics

CONTENTS

INTRODUCTION

 Life is short.

Time is precious.

There are only so many hours in the day.

You are probably familiar with these cliché expressions—no doubt because you used them yourself as excuses for ducking assigned reading of the classics.

Don't worry—we're not here to classics shame you (although maybe you should feel just a *little* guilty). We want to help you bone up on what you missed while frittering away your time on less literary endeavors. *TL;DR Literature* (that acronym stands for *Too Long; Didn't Read*) is not only the corrective that you want—it's the resource that you need to get a grip on what you let slip. It distills thirteen classics

of twentieth-century literature down to their essential elements: plot summary, character descriptions, and explanations of significant dramatic moments in the stories. What's more, it embellishes its pithy particulars with illustrative infographics to help fix each novel's narrative in your mind's eye. After all, we know that a picture is worth a thousand words—and it was their thousands of words that deterred you from reading these books in the first place.

We've gone one step further and organized the contents into thematically oriented divisions that will encourage you to consider why diverse authors from widely varied backgrounds were drawn to certain ideas resonant in their time and culture. The four divisions are as follows:

IF THIS GOES ON

Although some consider that we live in the best of all possible worlds, a number of writers have pondered the worst possibilities of idealized societies. Aldous Huxley, in *Brave New World*, presents a future dystopia where sexual liberation and detachment from familial affiliations have rendered people soulless. Conversely, in Margaret Atwood's *The Handmaid's Tale*, control of reproductive rights is a tool wielded cruelly by an overbearing theocratic order. In Ray Bradbury's *Fahrenheit 451*, it is the job of firemen to burn books to help keep society docile and focused on frivolous activities that frustrate serious thought. Similarly, in George Orwell's *1984*, free thought and speech are denied by a government that rewrites the historical record to control any contradiction of its pernicious objectives.

MADE IN AMERICA

The concept of "the American Dream" has long fascinated writers, who have attempted to define it and what it represents by approaching it from a variety of different perspectives. In John Steinbeck's *Of Mice and Men*, that dream is the hope that two farm workers have of eventually finding the means to own property and enjoy financial independence at the height of the Great Depression. In *The Great Gatsby*, F. Scott Fitzgerald views the same dream from another angle: its eponymous character is a self-made man who learns that, for all of his extravagant wealth, he cannot buy the one thing that he desires most. Arthur Miller, in his drama *The Crucible*, shines a light on a defining American

event, the Salem witch trials, to explore ideas of personal honor and social persecution that are still relevant today. And in Tim O'Brien's mosaic novel, *The Things They Carried*, the private dreams of its characters collide with the nightmare of the overseas war they struggle to survive as soldiers.

🦅

RACE AND IDENTITY

Issues of race and ethnicity inform some of the twentieth century's most distinguished works of literature. The novels grouped in this section all explore how race shapes the indi-

vidual identities of their characters and the culture they are part of. The main character in Zora Neale Hurston's *Their Eyes Were Watching God* is a woman of color seeking personal independence in an American south where slavery is still a recent memory and where women are expected to be subservient to their husbands and defined by their marriage to them. In Harper Lee's *To Kill a Mockingbird*, a young white girl growing up in Depression-era Alabama awakens to an understanding of racial inequality and the injustice of judging someone by the color of their skin or racial heritage. Chinua Achebe, in *Things Fall Apart*, brings a global perspective to racial matters in his account of an African male trying to live by the code of his tribe in a nation being transformed by rampant European colonialism.

BOYS WILL BE BOYS

Boys certainly *will* be boys, and the novels selected for this section approach the boyhoods of their characters from radically different perspectives. Holden Caulfield, the narrator of J. D. Salinger's *The Catcher in the Rye*, is a young man who clings so tenaciously to his childhood and its comforting trappings of innocence that it impedes his transition to the world of adulthood—making it a sort of "*not*-coming-of-age" novel. And in *Lord of the Flies*, William Golding finds in a group of young schoolboys marooned on an isolated island in the Pacific Ocean, independent of adult supervision and outside the bounds of civilization, a perfect study for humanity's descent into primitivism and savagery.

The chapters in *TL;DR Literature* provide quick study guides and serve as a useful refresher reference—but, of course, there's no substitute for reading the classics themselves. This book is designed to inspire readers to seek out the original works and discover first-hand why they are regarded as masterpieces of literature.

BRAVE NEW WORLD

1984

FAHRENHEIT 451

THE HANDMAID'S TALE

BRAVE NEW WORLD

Genre:
Dystopian fiction;
Science fiction

Setting:
England and New Mexico
in 2540 AD

Year Published:
1932

Author:
Aldous Huxley

ALPHAS
BETAS
GAMMAS
DELTAS
EPSILONS

In telling the story of a civilization where suffering and pain have been eradicated at the price of personal autonomy, *Brave New World* explores the dehumanizing effects of technology, and implies that pain is necessary for life to have meaning. It is set in a future where advanced reproductive technologies are used to dissociate individuals from the emotional bonds of family and sexual partners and to program people as members of rigidly defined social castes based on their intellect or capacity for labor.

Plot Overview

Climax: After Linda dies, John incites a riot in the hospital when he tries to free people from their dependence on the happiness-inducing drug, *soma*.

Rising Action: Bernard asks Lenina on a date to visit a Savage Reservation. There they meet Linda, and her son John, who has been raised outside of the programmed society. Linda and John return with Bernard and Lenina to the World State.

Falling Action: John isolates himself in a lighthouse and punishes himself. A crowd finds him and, after he succumbs to sexual temptation, he hangs himself.

Major Conflict: The idealistic utopia of the World State fails to satisfy the longings of its members.

Main Characters

Bernard Marx: An Alpha male who holds unorthodox beliefs; the novel's central figure before John arrives.

Lenina Crowne: A vaccination worker whom many characters desire.

Helmholtz Watson: An Alpha lecturer who longs to create something meaningful.

John (aka the "Savage"): The central protagonist and son of the Director and Linda; an outsider to the World State.

Linda: John's mother, who got stranded on the Reservation many years earlier.

The Director: The threatening administrator of the Central London Hatchery and Conditioning Centre.

Mustapha Mond: The most powerful and intelligent proponent of the World State.

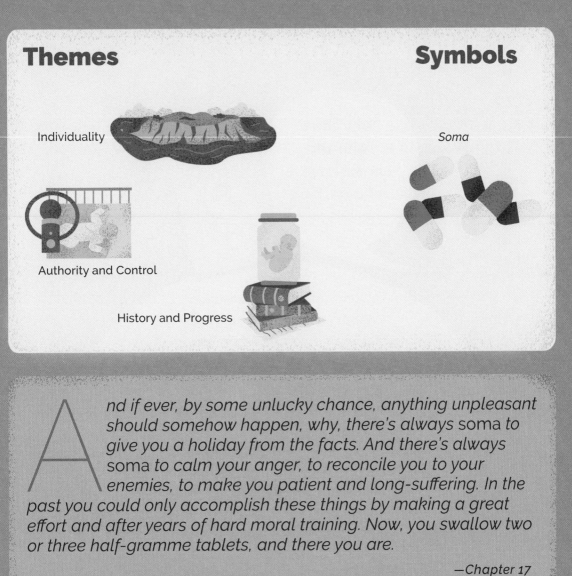

Themes

Individuality

Authority and Control

History and Progress

Symbols

Soma

A nd if ever, by some unlucky chance, anything unpleasant should somehow happen, why, there's always soma *to give you a holiday from the facts. And there's always* soma *to calm your anger, to reconcile you to your enemies, to make you patient and long-suffering. In the past you could only accomplish these things by making a great effort and after years of hard moral training. Now, you swallow two or three half-gramme tablets, and there you are.*

—Chapter 17

Key Question and Answer

Why can't John and Lenina have a relationship?

WHY ?

John grew up on the Savage Reservation, where traditional monogamy is enforced. John wants to "do something" romantic for Lenina. Lenina, on the other hand, grew up in the World State. She believes that it is morally wrong to be monogamous, or to delay pleasure. She wants to have sex with John right away. Lenina thinks it makes no sense to wait before having sex, while John thinks it is disgusting not to wait. Even though they are attracted to one another, they can't find common ground about what a relationship ought to be.

What Does the Ending Mean?

Huxley repeatedly emphasizes the incompatibility of happiness and truth. Throughout the novel, John has argued that it's better to seek truth, even if it involves suffering, than to accept an easy life of pleasure and happiness. However, when Mustapha Mond grants him the freedom to seek truth through self-sacrifice and suffering, John succumbs to the temptation of physical pleasure and hangs himself out of shame. This ending might suggest that the happiness encouraged by the World State's Controllers is a more powerful force than the truth John seeks; or, that John has failed in his search for truth because the Controllers have made it impossible to avoid the temptation of happiness.

1984

Genre:
Dystopian fiction;
Science fiction

Setting:
Oceania

Year Published:
1949

Author:
George Orwell

1984 follows the life of Winston Smith, whose personal desires collide with the ruling Party's ideology and raise the stakes of how far he will go to maintain his autonomy. *1984* ultimately explores the dangers of totalitarianism and warns against a world governed by propaganda, surveillance, and censorship. The Party figurehead, Big Brother, is an all-seeing dictator who demands the undying devotion of Oceania's citizens. Winston works in the Ministry of Truth where his job entails revising the historical record to suit the Party's needs.

Plot Overview

Rising Action: Winston and Julia begin their affair; O'Brien falsely claims he's a member of the rebellious Brotherhood that hopes to overthrow Big Brother. Winston and Julia are arrested by the Party.

Climax: O'Brien tortures Winston with the cage of rats and Winston chooses Big Brother over Julia.

Falling Action: Winston reintegrates back into society as a loyal Party member, and he and Julia realize they betrayed each other under torture.

I LOVE YOU

Major Conflict: Winston and Julia struggle against the dehumanizing policies of the Party, and must choose between individuality and conformity.

Main Characters

Winston: The protagonist who hates the Party and wants to test the limits of its power.

Big Brother: The perceived ruler of Oceania.

O'Brien: A mysterious and powerful member of the Inner Party whom Winston believes is also a member of the Brotherhood.

Julia: Winston's lover and the only other person who Winston can be sure hates the Party and wishes to rebel against it as he does.

Mr. Charrington: An old man who runs a secondhand store in the prole district and is a member of the Thought Police.

Themes

Mind Control and Newspeak

Manipulation of History

Resistance and Revolution

Symbols

Big Brother

The Glass Paperweight

The Place Where There Is No Darkness

The Telescreens

The Red-Armed Prole Woman

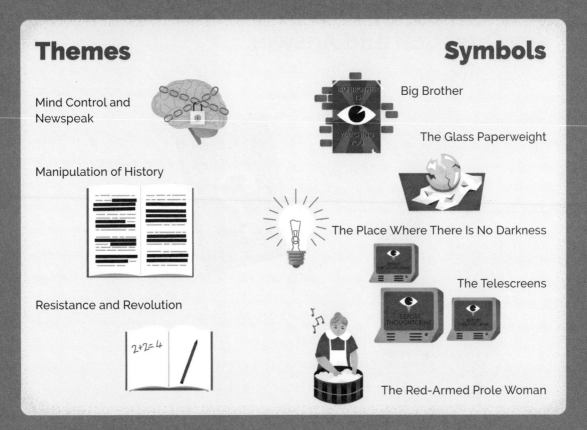

And when memory failed and written records were falsified—when that happened, the claim of the Party to have improved the conditions of human life had got to be accepted, because there did not exist, and never again could exist, any standard against which it could be tested.

—Part 1, Chapter 8

Key Question and Answer

Why does O'Brien pretend to be part of the Brotherhood?

WHY ?

O'Brien pretends to be part of the Brotherhood because he knows that deceiving Winston and Julia will make the eventual process of controlling their minds all the more powerful. O'Brien could have had them arrested when they came to his house and pledged allegiance to the Brotherhood and to taking down Big Brother, but he understood that allowing them to believe that there is hope for destroying the Party only to yank it away allows him to crush their spirits more easily.

What Does the Ending Mean?

The final chapter follows Winston for an afternoon some time following his release from the Ministry of Love. The reader learns that Winston now leads a life of easy, meaningless work, and that when he spoke to Julia again, she admitted that she had also turned on Winston. The two now feel nothing for each other. In the final moment of the novel, Winston encounters an image of Big Brother and experiences a sense of victory rather than self-defeat. Winston's total acceptance of Party rule marks the completion of the trajectory he has been on since the opening of the novel. His acknowledgment in the novel's final line that he loves Big Brother signals his total capitulation to the Party.

FAHRENHEIT 451

Genre:
Dystopian fiction;
Speculative fiction

Setting:
The United States, in an
unreported future time

Year Published:
1953

Author:
Ray Bradbury

Fahrenheit 451 tells the story of Guy Montag and his transformation from a book-burning fireman to a book-reading rebel. Montag lives in an oppressive society that attempts to eliminate all sources of complexity, contradiction, and confusion to ensure uncomplicated happiness for all its citizens. As Montag comes to realize over the course of the novel, however, his fellow citizens are not happy so much as selfish and hollow. The novel's title is explained as "the temperature at which book paper catches fire, and burns."

Plot Overview

Climax: The women turn Montag in to the firemen, and Montag sets Captain Beatty on fire and flees.

Rising Action: Montag grows conscious of the problems in his society after meeting Clarisse McClellan; Montag steals a book that he was supposed to burn, and Captain Beatty warns him against reading; Montag upsets his wife Mildred and her friends when he reads a book aloud.

Falling Action: Montag goes to the country where he meets a band of intellectuals committed to memorizing books. Eventually, a bomb destroys the city.

Major Conflict: Guy Montag struggles against a society that grows increasingly selfish, pleasure-seeking, disconnected, and empty.

Main Characters

Professor Faber: A retired English professor who berates himself for being a coward but shows himself capable of acts that require great courage.

Guy Montag: A fireman who suddenly realizes the emptiness of his life and starts to search for meaning in the books he is supposed to be burning.

Mildred Montag: Montag's wife, who is obsessed with watching television and refuses to talk to Montag about their marriage or her feelings.

Clarisse McClellan: A seventeen-year-old who introduces Montag to the world's potential for beauty and meaning with her gentle innocence and curiosity.

Captain Beatty: The captain of Montag's fire department, who is well-read, but hates books and people who insist on reading them.

Granger: The leader of the "Book People," the group of hobo intellectuals Montag finds in the country.

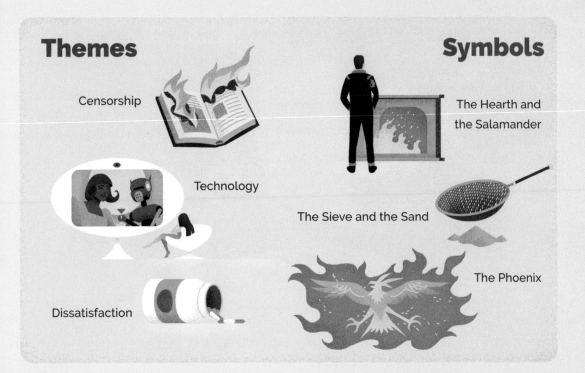

Themes

Censorship

Technology

Dissatisfaction

Symbols

The Hearth and
the Salamander

The Sieve and the Sand

The Phoenix

> ow like a mirror, too, her face. Impossible; for how many people did you know that refracted your own light to you? People were more often—he searched for a simile, found one in his work—torches, blazing away until they whiffed out.
>
> —*The Hearth and the Salamander*

Key Question and Answer

Why did the government ban books?

WHY
?

According to Beatty's account, books slowly fell out of favor over the course of several decades when technological advancement proceeded at an ever-quickening pace. As the speed of life accelerated, people increasingly opted for simplified forms of entertainment, like television. Fast-paced living and shallow entertainment worked together to erode people's attention spans. Society evolved in a way that privileged happiness above all else. Books, however, threatened to undermine this ideal of happiness by introducing unnecessary complexity into people's lives. Books were feared because they brought confusion and discontent.

What Does the Ending Mean?

The novel ends with Montag escaping the city in the midst of a new declaration of war. Once he's in the country, Montag meets a band of roving intellectuals who have elected to preserve significant works of literature in their memory. Soon after these people welcome Montag into their community, an atomic bomb falls on the city, reducing it to rubble and ash. This ending depicts the inevitable self-destruction of such an oppressive society, yet also offers a specter of hope. Now that he's in the country, Montag has the leisure to think for himself for the first time in his life. Furthermore, despite having believed that he and Faber were the only citizens committed to resisting the firemen, Montag now finds that an entire community of rebels already exists. Montag will help lead the charge to rebuild his old community, the one that has just so violently annihilated itself.

THE HANDMAID'S TALE

Genre:
Dystopian fiction;
Speculative fiction

Setting: The Republic of
Gilead, a theocratic state
based in Cambridge,
Massachusetts

Year Published:
1985

Author:
Margaret Atwood

The Handmaid's Tale is set in a future America that has been overthrown by a fanatical religious group, the Sons of Jacob, who institute a patriarchal dictatorship that suppresses civil rights—especially the rights of women. It tells the story of Offred, a "Handmaid" who lives in the Republic of Gilead (the new name for America) and who has been subjugated and reduced to sexual slavery. Offred desires happiness and freedom, and finds herself struggling against the totalitarian restrictions of her society. As a Handmaid—one of the few sexually fertile women in the despoiled world of Gilead—Offred's role is to produce offspring for Gilead's leaders, the Commanders.

Plot Overview

Climax: After learning that Ofglen committed suicide to avoid arrest, Offred returns home from a shopping trip and Serena confronts her about her trip to Jezebel's.

Rising Action: Offred lives with the Commander and his wife, Serena Joy; Ofglen (a neighbor) tells Offred about an underground organization seeking to overthrow Gilead; Offred goes with the Commander to a club called Jezebel's; Offred and Nick (the Commander's chauffer) have sex, at Serena's suggestion.

Falling Action: Offred is taken away in a van filled with Eyes, and she's unsure if she's escaping or being arrested.

Major Conflict: Offred struggles to preserve her sense of self and humanity under the oppressive regime of the Republic of Gilead.

Main Characters

Aunt Lydia: One of the "Aunts" responsible for Offred's "re-education" at the Red Center, who states some of the most misogynistic and distorted ideas in the novel.

The Commander: The head of the household where Offred works as a Handmaid, who initiates an unorthodox relationship with her.

Serena Joy: The Commander's wife, who sits at the top of the female social ladder, yet is desperately unhappy.

Ofglen: A Handmaid who is Offred's shopping partner and a member of the subversive "Mayday" underground.

Offred: The narrator and protagonist of *The Handmaid's Tale*, who shares the physical and psychological burdens of her daily life as a Handmaid.

Nick: A Guardian assigned to the Commander's home, who has a covert affair with Offred.

Janine: A conformist Handmaid Offred knows from the Red Center.

Moira: Offred's best friend from college, who is a resourceful and independent feminist.

Luke: Offred's former husband whom she remembers lovingly, and feels anguish for when she cannot preserve her memory of him.

Themes

Gender Roles

Imprisonment

Language and Power

Symbols

Harvard University

The Handmaid's Red Habits

The Eyes

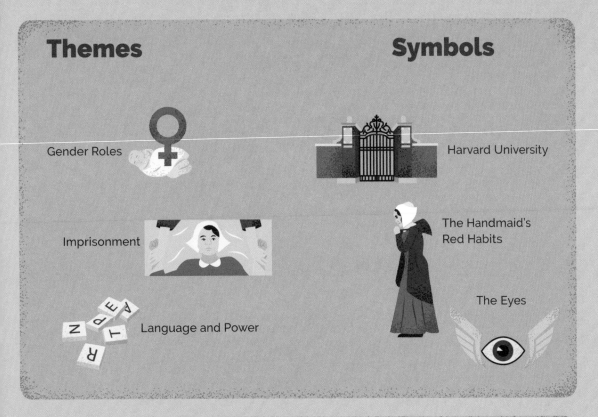

My name isn't Offred, I have another name, which nobody uses now because it's forbidden. I tell myself it doesn't matter, your name is like your telephone number, useful only to others; but what I tell myself is wrong, it does matter.

—Chapter 14

Key Question and Answer

What happened to Offred's daughter?

WHY ?

The story of Offred's daughter is related to us in snatches, conveying the sense that Offred cannot bear to think about her daughter for too long at a time. Over the course of the novel we learn that mother and daughter were separated when they were caught trying to escape the country. While Offred was taken to the Red Center, her daughter was rehomed with an infertile couple. Offred does not learn that this is what has happened to her daughter until Serena Joy shows Offred a picture of the now nearly grown girl.

What Does the Ending Mean?

Offred is ushered out of the Commander's house by the Eyes of God (i.e., secret police nicknamed "the Eyes"), who may or may not be members of the rebel group Mayday. In the final "Historical Notes" section, we learn that the Eyes were indeed members of Mayday. An academic, Dr. Piexoto, explains that the novel we have read is a transcript of a tape recording, discovered many years after the Gileadean era has come to an end. The ending of Offred's story emphasizes her passivity. She never takes a stand against the Gileadean regime. She escapes only because Nick, a rebel, needs to protect himself. However, the "Historical Notes" section underscores that despite her passivity, Offred's experience has value.

THE GREAT GATSBY

OF MICE AND MEN

THE CRUCIBLE

THE THINGS THEY CARRIED

THE GREAT GATSBY

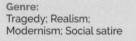

Genre:
Tragedy; Realism;
Modernism; Social satire

Setting:
Long Island and
New York City

Year Published:
1925

Author:
F. Scott Fitzgerald

The Great Gatsby is a story about the impossibility of recapturing the past and the difficulty of altering one's future. Jay Gatsby is the mysterious and wealthy neighbor of the narrator, Nick Carraway. As the novel progresses and Nick becomes increasingly drawn into Gatsby's complicated world, the reader learns what Gatsby wants: Daisy, Nick's cousin, the girl he once loved. Daisy's brutish husband Tom, class difference, societal expectations, and Gatsby's past lies work to thwart Gatsby's dream.

Plot Overview

Rising Action: Jay Gatsby throws lavish parties and arranges a meeting with Daisy Buchanan at Nick Carraway's house.

Climax: Gatsby reunites with Daisy, and Gatsby and Tom, Daisy's husband, confront each other in the Plaza Hotel.

Falling Action: Daisy rejects Gatsby, Daisy hits Myrtle Wilson with Gatsby's car, and George Wilson, mistaking Gatsby as the driver, kills Gatsby.

Major Conflict: Gatsby has amassed a vast fortune in order to win the affections of the upper-class Daisy Buchanan, but his mysterious past stands in the way of his being accepted by her.

Main Characters

Daisy Buchanan: Nick's cousin who reunites with lovelorn Gatsby, arousing the jealousy of Tom.

Nick Carraway: The novel's narrator who facilitates the rekindling of Gatsby and Daisy's romance.

Tom Buchanan: Daisy's wealthy husband who has an affair with Myrtle, but confronts Gatsby about his relationship with Daisy.

Jay Gatsby: The title character and protagonist who throws lavish parties and dedicates himself to winning Daisy back from Tom.

Jordan Baker: Daisy's friend with whom Nick becomes romantically involved.

Myrtle Wilson: Tom's mistress who feels imprisoned by her marriage to George.

George Wilson: Myrtle's husband, who owns a garage in the valley of ashes.

Themes

The American Dream

Love and Marriage

The Role of the Past

Symbols

(1) The Green Light
(2) The Valley of Ashes
(3) The Eyes of Doctor T.J. Eckleburg

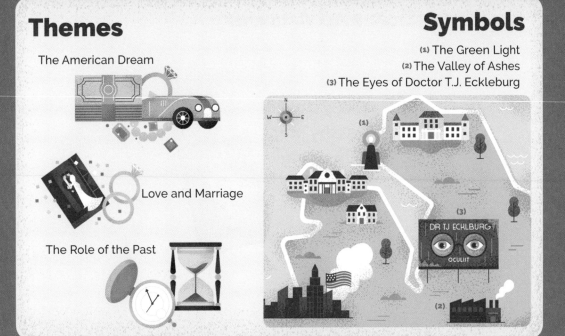

He talked a lot about the past, and I gathered that he wanted to recover something, some idea of himself perhaps, that had gone into loving Daisy.

—Chapter 6

Key Question and Answer

Why does Gatsby stop throwing parties?

After Daisy and Tom finally attend one of Gatsby's parties, Gatsby abruptly stops throwing them, for there no longer is a reason to hold such events. As soon as he reunites with Daisy and she has seen proof of Gatsby's wealth, he doesn't feel the need to show it off anymore.

What Does the Ending Mean?

Although the main events of the novel end with Gatsby's murder and George Wilson's suicide, *The Great Gatsby* concludes with a chapter in which Nick reflects on the aftermath of Gatsby's death. Nick links the American Dream to Gatsby's love for Daisy, commenting on the unattainable nature of both. Pondering Gatsby's fate, Nick muses, "his dream must have seemed so close that he could hardly fail to grasp it. He did not know that it was already behind him, somewhere back in that vast obscurity beyond the city, where the dark fields of the republic rolled on under the night." Hence the novel's famous final line: "So we beat on, boats against the current, borne back ceaselessly into the past."

OF MICE AND MEN

Genre:
Social realist fiction

Setting:
California in the 1930s

Year Published:
1937

Author:
John Steinbeck

Of Mice and Men tells the story of the friendship between George Milton, an uneducated but quick-witted farm worker, and Lennie Small, a physically strong but mentally challenged friend whom George has known and protected since childhood. That friendship is tested by the isolating and predatory reality of life for poor migrant workers in Depression-era America. Their dream of one day purchasing a farm together is complicated by Lennie's inability to stay out of trouble on the job, and George's inability to stay angry at Lennie long enough to leave and find work on his own.

Plot Overview

Climax: Lennie, underestimating his strength, accidentally kills Curley's wife in the barn.

Falling Action: Lennie runs away; Curley leads a mob of men to search for and kill Lennie; George finds Lennie and, while retelling the story of life on their farm, shoots him in the back of the head to save him from Curley's lynch mob.

Rising Action: George and Lennie report for work on a ranch where Curley, the boss's son, picks on Lennie. George and Lennie befriend the other ranch-hands, especially Candy.

Major Conflict: George and Lennie, two migrant workers and friends, struggle to overcome their oppressive, impoverished circumstances and become financially stable enough to own land together.

Main Characters

George: A small, quick-witted man who travels with, and cares for, Lennie.

Lennie: A large, childlike migrant worker who loves to pet soft things, is blindly devoted to George and their vision of the farm, and possesses incredible physical strength.

Candy: An aging ranch handyman, who seizes on George's description of the farm he and Lennie will own, offering his life's savings if he can join.

Curley's Wife: The only female character in the story, who represents the temptation of female sexuality in a male-dominated world, but who is desperately lonely.

Curley: The boss's son, who is a confrontational, mean-spirited, and aggressive young man who picks fights with larger men.

Slim: A skilled mule driver and the acknowledged "prince" of the ranch, whom the other characters often turn to for advice.

Crooks: The proud yet bitter black stable-hand, who is isolated from the other men because of the color of his skin.

Carlson: A ranch-hand, who convinces Candy to put his old dog out of its misery.

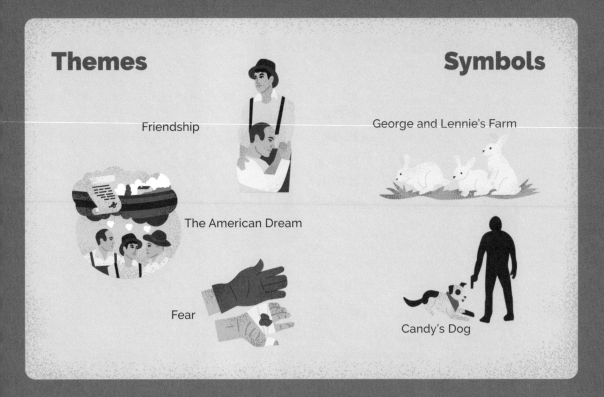

Themes

Friendship

The American Dream

Fear

Symbols

George and Lennie's Farm

Candy's Dog

> *S*omeday—we're gonna get the jack together and we're gonna have a little house and a couple of acres an' a cow and some pigs and—"
>
> "An' live off the fatta the lan'," *Lennie shouted.* "An' have rabbits. *Go on, George!*"
>
> —Of Mice and Men

Key Question and Answer

Why does Curley attack Lennie?

After Slim denies Curley's accusation that he was hanging around Curley's wife, Curley looks to take his anger out on an easier target, and chooses Lennie. Lennie is "smiling with delight" as he dreams about the future farm, ignorant that he is attracting Curley's humiliated anger. By picking on Lennie, Curley demonstrates that he is willing to prey on the most vulnerable in order to maintain his dominance over the workers. *Of Mice and Men* suggests that this is one way that the property-owning classes uphold their power.

What Does the Ending Mean?

George must choose between mercifully killing the friend he loves with his own hands, or allowing Lennie's inevitable lynching by a mob that does not care about Lennie's fate. George spares Lennie from Curley's wrath by shooting Lennie in the back of the head after reciting their shared dream of owning a farm one final time. Because George is forced to kill his friend himself, Lennie's death is not only the death of a single vulnerable person, but also the destruction of a rare and idealized friendship. George and Lennie's dream of owning a farm, which would have enabled them to sustain themselves, and offer them protection from an inhospitable world, represents a prototypically American ideal. Their journey, which awakens George to the impossibility of this dream, sadly proves that such paradises of freedom, contentment, and safety are not to be found in this world.

THE CRUCIBLE

Genre:
Tragedy; Allegory;
Historical drama

Setting:
Salem, Massachusetts

Year Published:
1953

Author:
Arthur Miller

In telling the story of a seventeenth-century New England town so gripped by hysteria that they kill many of their own residents, *The Crucible* explores the tension between the repressive forces of social order and individual freedom. The residents of Salem temporarily lose their sense of community and vilify one another, succumbing to the hysteria of the witch hunts. Arthur Miller wrote this play at the height of America's McCarthy era, using the Salem witch trials as an allegory for Red Scare prosecutions.

Plot Overview

Climax: John tells the Salem court that he committed adultery with Abigail Williams.

Rising Action: A group of young girls, including Abigail Williams, dance with the slave Tituba in the forest. Abigail accuses Elizabeth Proctor, John Proctor's wife, of witchcraft. John is hesitant to testify for fear of revealing his affair with Abigail.

Falling Action: John chooses to die rather than sign his name to his confession of practicing witchcraft.

Major Conflict: Salem falls apart as fear mounts over the witch hunts, and John Proctor wrestles with his personal morality.

Main Characters

Abigail Williams: A manipulative girl with whom John Proctor had an affair.

John Proctor: The protagonist, a reputable farmer and husband who hides his affair with Abigail Williams.

Elizabeth Proctor: John Proctor's virtuous wife.

Judge Danforth: The deputy governor of Massachusetts and the presiding judge at the witch trials.

Reverend John Hale: A young minister reputed to be an expert on witchcraft.

Giles Corey: An elderly but feisty farmer in Salem, famous for his tendency to file lawsuits.

Mary Warren: The servant in the Proctor household and a member of Abigail's group of girls.

Thomas Putnam: An influential citizen of Salem who uses the witch trials to build his wealth.

Rebecca Nurse: A wise and upright woman, held in tremendous regard by most of the Salem community.

Reverend Parris: The paranoid minister of Salem's church.

Themes

Symbols

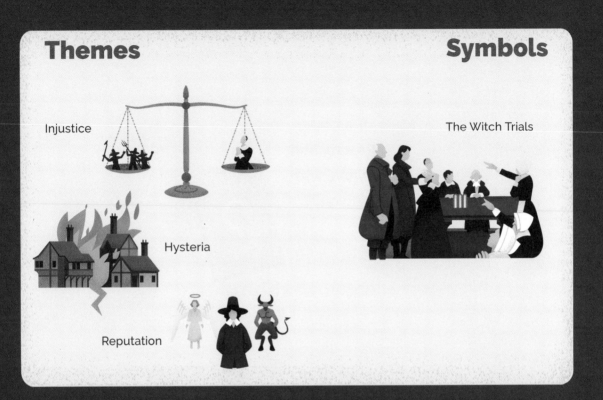

Injustice

Hysteria

Reputation

The Witch Trials

This is a sharp time, now, a precise time—we live no longer in the dusky afternoon when evil mixed itself with good and befuddled the world. Now, by God's grace, the shining sun is up, and them that fear not light will surely praise it.

—*Act 3*

Key Question and Answer

Was John Proctor still in love with Abigail?

WHY ?

John's feelings for Abigail are not entirely clear at the beginning of the play. He spends time with her in the first act, but he also makes it clear that he is not going to resume their affair. In the third act, John does indeed tell the court about his affair with Abigail to try to save Elizabeth. This confession seems to indicate that, if John ever loved Abigail, he loves Elizabeth much more. John has already realized he should not have cheated on his wife with Abigail, but he doesn't believe Elizabeth at first when she tells him Abigail wants her dead. By the end of the play, he believes Elizabeth, and hates Abigail.

What Does the Ending Mean?

After having signed, then ripped up his confession, John Proctor declares that he cannot throw away his good name in a lie, even though doing so would save his life. He chooses to die. The ending resolves the question of whether or not John Proctor will prove to be a good man. Throughout the play, John has made both good and bad moral choices. He initially signs a confession even though he knows in his heart that it's wrong to do so and refuses to save himself even when Putnam and Parris, fearing an uprising among Salem's citizens, beg him. In the end, John's refusal to dishonor himself, even at the cost of his own life, shows that he is ultimately a good man. The price of this goodness is death. As Elizabeth says, he can "have his goodness now" and she won't take it from him.

THE THINGS THEY CARRIED

Genre:
War novel;
Linked short stories

Setting:
Vietnam during the
Vietnam War

Year Published:
1990

Author:
Tim O'Brien

The Things They Carried is a collection of interconnected short stories that tell of Tim O'Brien's quest to understand his time in Vietnam, and how that experience changed and shaped him and his friends. The stories catalog the variety of things his fellow soldiers in the Alpha Company brought on their missions. Several of these things are intangible, including guilt and fear, while others are specific physical objects, including matches, morphine, M-16 rifles, and M&M's candy. Several of the stories are told from a perspective twenty years after the Vietnam War, when O'Brien is a forty-three-year-old writer living in Massachusetts.

Plot Overview

Climax: During their tour of duty, the men of the Alpha Company must cope with the loss of their own men and the guilt that comes from watching others die—especially a young Vietnamese soldier whom O'Brien believes he killed.

Rising Action: In the summer of 1968, Tim O'Brien receives a draft notice. Despite a desire to follow his convictions and flee to Canada, he feels he would be embarrassed to refuse to fulfill his patriotic duty and so concedes to fight in Vietnam.

Falling Action: After he returns from war, O'Brien grapples with his memories by telling stories about Vietnam.

Major Conflict: The men of the Alpha Company, especially Tim O'Brien, contend with the effects—both immediate and long-term—of the Vietnam War.

Main Characters

Tim O'Brien: The narrator and protagonist of the collection, who tells stories to deal with his guilt and confusion over the atrocities he witnessed in Vietnam.

Jimmy Cross: The lieutenant of the Alpha Company, who is responsible for the entire group of men and becomes wracked with guilt upon believing he caused the deaths of two soldiers.

Mitchell Sanders: One of the most likable soldiers in the company, whose ability to tell stories and discuss their nuances makes a profound impression on O'Brien.

Kiowa: O'Brien's closest friend and a model of quiet, rational morality amid the atrocities of war.

Norman Bowker: A member of the Alpha Company who embodies the damage that the war can do to a soldier long after the war is over.

Henry Dobbins: The platoon's machine gunner and resident gentle giant.

Bob "Rat" Kiley: The platoon's medic, who eventually succumbs to the stresses of war by purposely blowing off his toe.

Curt Lemon: A childish and careless member of the Alpha Company who is killed when he steps on a rigged mortar round.

Ted Lavender: A young, scared soldier in the Alpha Company, who is the first to die.

Elroy Berdahl: The proprietor of the Tip Top Lodge near the Canadian border, who serves as the closest thing to a father figure for O'Brien.

Kathleen: O'Brien's daughter and a symbol of the naïve outsider.

Mary Anne Bell: One soldier's high school sweetheart, who arrives in Vietnam full of innocence, but succumbs to the darkness of the jungle and, according to legend, disappears there.

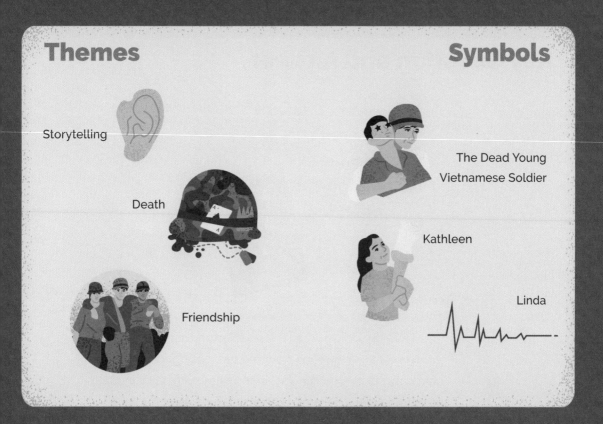

Themes

Storytelling

Death

Friendship

Symbols

The Dead Young Vietnamese Soldier

Kathleen

Linda

y telling stories, you objectify your own experience. You separate it from yourself. You pin down certain truths. You make up others.

—*Notes*

Key Question and Answer

Why aren't the stories in chronological order?

WHY
?

The narrator of the novel, Tim, tells the stories that the novel comprises to try to understand how the war changed him, and to remember the friends he made (and sometimes lost) there. Thus, he is more interested in the recurring ideas, themes, and images of the war than in recreating the factual chronology of the war. The fractured, repetitious, and occasionally confusing flow of stories in the novel reflects Tim's experience in Vietnam, as well as how he thinks about it in the present.

What Does the Ending Mean?

The book ends with a story titled "The Lives of the Dead," in which Tim remembers his childhood love, Linda, who died of cancer when she was 9. Tim says that in a story, he can bring Linda back to life. Tim realizes that this is what he has done for the other dead characters in the book, including Ted Lavender, Dave Jensen, Kiowa, and the dead young Vietnamese man. He has kept them alive by writing about them. Tim realizes that while he cannot live forever, he can save his own life by telling the story of what happened to him in Vietnam. Not only will he save others who have died by remembering them in his writing, but the act of writing will save him, too.

THEIR EYES WERE WATCHING GOD

TO KILL A MOCKINGBIRD

THINGS FALL APART

THEIR EYES WERE WATCHING GOD

Genre:
Bildungsroman

Setting:
Rural Florida

Year Published:
1937

Author:
Zora Neale Hurston

Their Eyes Were Watching God tells the story of Janie Crawford's passage from repression to spiritual fulfillment as she clashes with the expectations thrust upon her by others. Inspired by the revelation she received as a teenager, Janie elevates marriage and love in her mind as the highest achievement, but this ideal is defiled when she marries Logan Killicks, and later Jody Starks, two men whom she does not love. It is not until she meets Tea Cake that Janie experiences a joyful relationship, and she ultimately achieves self-actualization after Tea Cake saves her from a rabid dog and sacrifices his own life for her sake.

Plot Overview

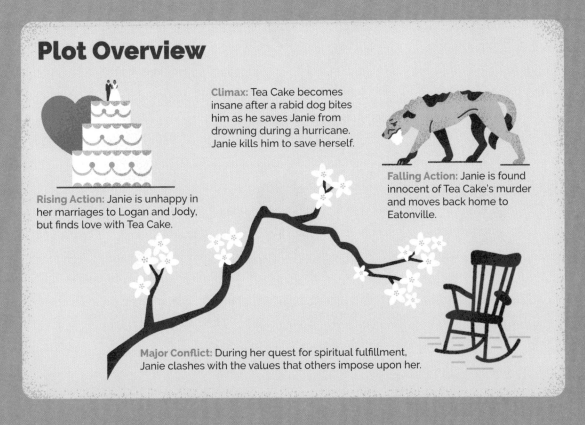

Climax: Tea Cake becomes insane after a rabid dog bites him as he saves Janie from drowning during a hurricane. Janie kills him to save herself.

Falling Action: Janie is found innocent of Tea Cake's murder and moves back home to Eatonville.

Rising Action: Janie is unhappy in her marriages to Logan and Jody, but finds love with Tea Cake.

Major Conflict: During her quest for spiritual fulfillment, Janie clashes with the values that others impose upon her.

Main Characters

Tea Cake: Janie's third husband and first real love.

Janie Crawford: The novel's protagonist who overcomes racism and sexism to find self-actualization.

Jody Starks: Janie's second husband, an ambitious and power-hungry man.

Logan Killicks: The man Nanny arranges to be Janie's first husband.

Pheoby Watson: Janie's best friend in Eatonville.

Nanny Crawford: Janie's grandmother who has a strong concern for financial security.

Themes

Language: Speech and Silence

SHHH..

Power and Conquest

Love and Relationships vs. Independence

Symbols

The Hurricane

(1) Hair
(2) The Pear Tree
(3) The Horizon

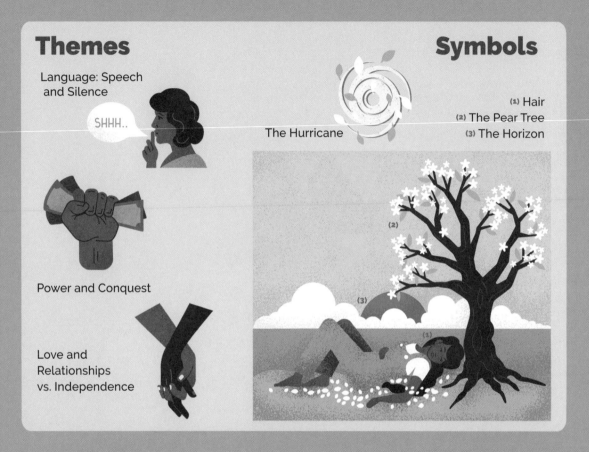

e drifted off to sleep and Janie looked down on him and felt a self-crushing love. So her soul crawled out from its hiding place.

—Chapter 13

Key Question and Answer

Why is the porch important?

The novel begins and ends on Janie's porch in Eatonville, which represents the community in *Their Eyes Were Watching God*. While porch-sitters in the novel are often misogynistic or nosy gossipers, Janie's place on the porch with Pheoby is a reminder that she has a place to tell her story.

What Does the Ending Mean?

A s a young girl, Janie sat beneath a pear tree and saw in the bees' interaction with it a perfect moment in nature, full of passionate intensity and blissful harmony. She has chased this ideal in her marriages throughout the book. Initially, Janie believed that Tea Cake's death would be "too much to bear," but in choosing to save her life, she affirms what she has been searching for since her revelation under the pear tree: self-actualization borne from true love. Not long after Janie clutches dead Tea Cake to her bosom and thanks "him wordlessly for giving her the chance for loving service," she must defend herself in court where the jury "all leaned over to listen while she talked." This conclusion to Janie's story greatly contrasts with her beginning, in which she strains to have her voice heard by Nanny, Logan, Jody, and many of her gossiping neighbors. The novel ends with Janie finally achieving what she always hoped for: "Here was peace."

TO KILL A MOCKINGBIRD

Genre:
Southern gothic;
Courtroom drama;
Bildungsroman

Setting:
Maycomb,
Alabama

Year Published:
1961

Author:
Harper Lee

To Kill a Mockingbird tells the story of Scout Finch's passage from innocence to experience when her father confronts the racist justice system of the rural, Depression-era South. In witnessing the trial of Tom Robinson, a black man unfairly accused of rape, Scout gains insight into her town, her family, and herself. Scout is forced to confront her beliefs, most significantly when Tom is convicted despite his clear innocence. Scout also faces her own prejudices through her encounters with Boo Radley, a mysterious shut-in. The novel's resolution comes when Boo rescues Scout and Jem and Scout realizes that Boo is a fully human, noble being. The novel's title is a reference to the destruction of innocence as it pertains to several of the characters. As Atticus tells Scout, "It's a sin to kill a mockingbird."

Plot Overview

Climax: The jury finds Tom Robinson guilty.

Rising Action: Scout, Jem, and Dill become fascinated with Boo Radley, and Atticus is assigned to defend Tom Robinson against Bob Ewell's charge that Tom raped his daughter Mayella.

Falling Action: When Bob Ewell assaults Scout and Jem, Boo Radley kills him.

Major Conflict: Scout and Jem grapple with the guilty verdict in Tom Robinson's trial and the vengefulness of Bob Ewell.

Main Characters

Atticus Finch: Scout and Jem's father, a lawyer who defends Tom Robinson.

Scout Finch: The novel's protagonist and narrator whose faith is tested by the prejudices of her community.

Jem Finch: Scout's brother who becomes disillusioned with the trial.

Bob Ewell: A drunken member of Maycomb's poorest family who accuses Tom Robinson of rape.

Arthur "Boo" Radley: A recluse who eventually saves Scout and Jem from harm.

Calpurnia: The Finch family's cook, a black woman, and a mother figure to Scout.

Themes

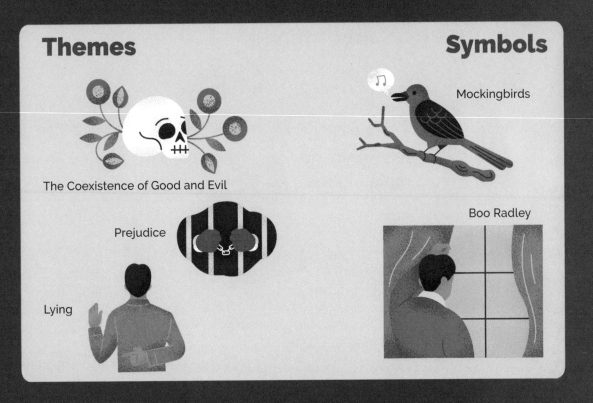

The Coexistence of Good and Evil

Prejudice

Lying

Symbols

Mockingbirds

Boo Radley

*Y*ou never really understand a person until you consider things from his point of view . . . until you climb into his skin and walk around in it.

—Chapter 3

Key Question and Answer

How is
Tom Robinson
a mockingbird?

WHY

?

The phrase
"it's a sin to kill a mockingbird" refers to
intentionally and pointlessly destroying
something that does no harm. When
the jury convicts Tom Robinson of rape
despite his innocence, the jury is guilty
of the same sort of
unnecessary cruelty.

What Does the Ending Mean?

When Bob Ewell attacks Jem and Scout as they walk home, Boo Radley intervenes and stabs Ewell fatally during the struggle. The sheriff, in order to protect Boo, insists that Ewell tripped over a tree root and fell on his own knife. After sitting with Scout for a while, Boo disappears once more into the Radley house. Later, Scout feels as though she can finally imagine what life is like for Boo. He has become a human being to her at last. With this realization, Scout embraces her father's advice to practice sympathy and understanding and demonstrates that her experiences with hatred and prejudice will not sully her faith in human goodness.

THINGS FALL APART

Genre:
Tragedy; Historical fiction

Setting:
Nigeria

Year Published:
1958

Author:
Chinua Achebe

Things Fall Apart tells the story of Okonkwo's ongoing obsession with his own masculinity. The novel chronicles his youth in Umuofia, his seven-year exile in Mbanta, and his eventual return home. Despite every attempt to gain status and become an exemplar of traditional Igbo masculinity, Okonkwo suffers from a feeling of relentless emasculation. His struggle to achieve recognition repeatedly draws him into conflict with his community, eventually leading both to his own downfall and to that of Umuofia and the nine villages. The novel's three parts map onto a gendered narrative structure that follows Okonkwo from his fatherland of Umuofia, to a motherland (Mbanta), and back to his fatherland. This gendered narrative structure functions in counterpoint with Okonkwo's ongoing obsession with his own masculinity.

Plot Overview

Climax: Okonkwo murders a court messenger.

Rising Action: Okonkwo participates in the killing of Ikemefuna; Enoch, a Christian convert, unmasks one of the egwugwu (ancestral spirits), who then burn down the Christian church. The District Commissioner sneakily arrests Umuofian leaders.

Falling Action: The villagers allow the white government's messengers to escape, and Okonkwo, realizing the weakness of his clan, commits suicide.

Major Conflict: On one level, the conflict is between the traditional society of Umuofia and the new customs brought by the white people, which are in turn adopted by many of the villagers. Okonkwo also struggles to be as different from his deceased father as possible.

Main Characters

Nwoye: Okonkwo's oldest son, who Okonkwo believes is weak and lazy.

Okonkwo: An influential leader in the Umuofia clan.

Ezinma: Okonkwo's favorite daughter and the only child of Okonkwo's second wife, Ekwefi.

Ikemefuna: A boy given to Okonkwo by a neighboring village.

Unoka: Okonkwo's father, of whom Okonkwo has been ashamed since childhood.

Uchendu: The younger brother of Okonkwo's mother who receives Okonkwo's family warmly in Mbanta.

The District Commissioner: A racist authority figure in the colonial government in Nigeria.

Mr. Brown: The first white missionary to travel to Umuofia.

Reverend James Smith: The strict missionary who replaces Mr. Brown.

Enoch: A fanatical convert to the Christian church in Umuofia.

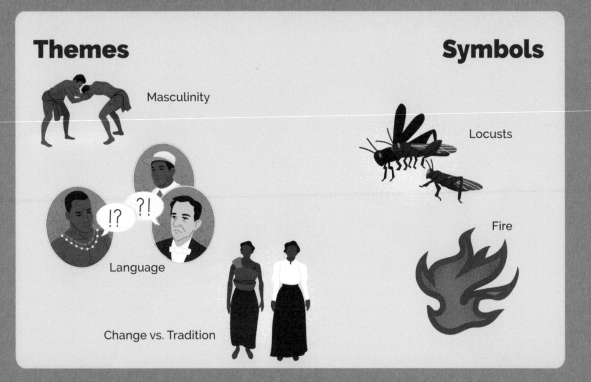

Themes

Masculinity

Language

Change vs. Tradition

Symbols

Locusts

Fire

Perhaps down in his heart Okonkwo was not a cruel man. But his whole life was dominated by fear, the fear of failure and of weakness.

—Chapter 2

Key Question and Answer

Why does Okonkwo kill Ikemefuna?

WHY ?

Okonkwo kills Ikemefuna because he doesn't want to appear weak in front of his fellow clansmen. Ogbuefi Ezeudu, a village elder, informs Okonkwo that the Oracle has decreed that Ikemefuna must be killed but that Okonkwo should not be the one to kill him, since Ikemefuna regards Okonkwo as a father. When Okonkwo and a group of clansmen take Ikemefuna to the woods to be killed, a clansman's blow fails to do the job, and the clansman yells to Okonkwo for help. Afraid of appearing weak, Okonkwo deals the fatal blow to Ikemefuna despite Ogbuefi Ezeudu's warning.

What Does the Ending Mean?

Things Fall Apart ends with two related tragedies. The first tragedy is Okonkwo's death. Following an outburst of unsanctioned violence in which he kills a European messenger who tries to stop a meeting among clan elders, Okonkwo realizes that he is no longer in sync with his society. Okonkwo retreats to his compound and hangs himself. With this act, Okonkwo lives up to his role as a tragic hero whose struggles with society ultimately lead to death. The novel's second tragedy occurs on the broader level of history. Achebe signals this second tragedy by ending the novel with a shift from an African to a European perspective. In the novel's final two pages, the District Commissioner reflects on how he will depict the events surrounding Okonkwo's death in the book he's working on, and he threatens to erase the specificity of Okonkwo's tragedy.

LORD OF THE FLIES

THE CATCHER IN THE RYE

LORD OF THE FLIES

Genre:
Dystopian fiction;
Allegorical fiction

Setting:
Deserted tropical
island

Year Published:
1954

Author:
William Golding

Lord of the Flies tells the story of a group of British boys marooned on an island, free from the rules that adult society formerly imposed on them. The boys struggle with the conflicting human instincts that exist within each of them—the instinct to work toward civilization and order and the instinct to descend into savagery, violence, and chaos. The novel's title—a name sometimes considered synonymous with that of Beelzebub, or Satan—references a sacrifice the boys make to the monster that they believe haunts the island, as well as to the evil inside them to which they give increasingly violent expression.

Plot Overview

Climax: When Simon tries to approach the other boys and tell them the Lord of the Flies is not a real beast, they kill Simon savagely, mistaking him for the beast.

Falling Action: The boys descend further into savagery and chaos. When the other boys kill Piggy and destroy the conch shell, Ralph flees from Jack's tribe and is saved from being killed by a rescuing naval officer on the beach.

Rising Action: When rumors surface that there is some sort of beast living on the island, the boys grow fearful, and the group begins to divide into two camps supporting Ralph and Jack, respectively.

Major Conflict: The boys marooned on the island struggle with the conflicting human instincts that exist within each of them.

Main Characters

Ralph: The novel's protagonist who is elected leader of the group of boys marooned on the island.

Jack: The novel's antagonist who becomes the leader of the hunters but longs for total power and becomes increasingly barbaric.

Roger: Jack's "lieutenant" who is a sadistic older boy.

Piggy: Ralph's "lieutenant" who represents the rational side of civilization.

Sam and Eric: A pair of twins closely allied with Ralph.

Simon: The only naturally "good" character who embodies a kind of innate morality that is deeply connected with nature.

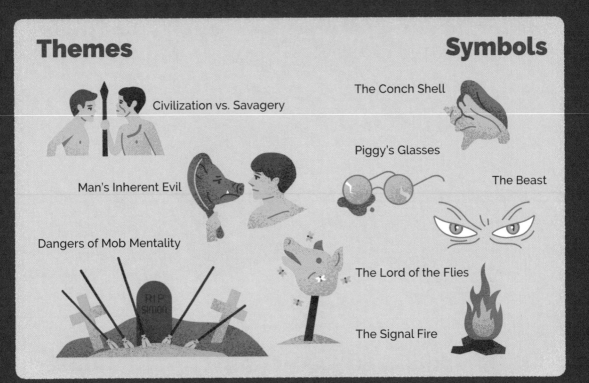

Themes

Civilization vs. Savagery

Man's Inherent Evil

Dangers of Mob Mentality

Symbols

The Conch Shell

Piggy's Glasses

The Beast

The Lord of the Flies

The Signal Fire

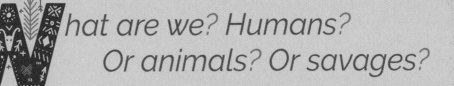

*What are we? Humans?
Or animals? Or savages?*

—Chapter 5

Key Question and Answer

Who is the Lord of the Flies?

WHY ?

The Lord of the Flies is the pig's head mounted on a sharpened stick and left as an offering for the beast. When the Lord of the Flies "speaks" to Simon, we can assume that his voice is a hallucinatory effect of Simon's disintegrating mental state. The Lord of the Flies suggests to Simon that the boys will be their own undoing. Symbolically, the Lord of the Flies represents the evil inside each one of the boys on the island.

What Does the Ending Mean?

After Jack and his followers kill Piggy, Ralph realizes that his life is in danger and flees to the forest. The fire that the boys set to flush Jack out catches the attention of a British naval officer on a passing ship who lands on the beach, where he discovers Ralph. Soon the rest of the boys join Ralph and tell the officer about their ordeal. As they speak, the reality of what has happened to them finally hits them. They are transformed from murderous savages back into scared children. However, the officer reminds readers that while the boys have been trying to survive and maintain civilization on the island, adults all over the world were waging war for no discernible reason.

THE CATCHER IN THE RYE

Genre:
Bildungsroman; Realism;
Literary satire

Setting:
Pennsylvania and
New York City

Year Published:
1951

Author:
J. D. Salinger

The Catcher in the Rye is the story of Holden Caulfield attempting to connect with other people and failing to do so, which causes him to dread maturity and cling to his idealized view of childhood. Holden's fear of growing up is evoked in the novel's title, a reference to his fantasy in which he envisions himself as a protector who keeps children playing in a field of rye from plummeting over a cliff. Because he has little sense of his effect on others and refuses to conform to societal norms, Holden fails in every attempt at connection, and adopts a self-protective veneer of disgust with the world.

Plot Overview

Climax: Holden visits his sister Phoebe, who becomes angry that Holden has been expelled from another school and confronts him about why he doesn't like anything.

Rising Action: Holden leaves Pencey Prep for New York City, where he has many experiences in which he wavers between interacting with other people as an adult and retreating from them as a child.

Falling Action: Holden decides to run away for good, but his plan collapses when Phoebe insists on coming with him; Holden watches Phoebe riding a carousel, secure for the moment in her innocence; Holden looks toward his future with acceptance.

Major Conflict: Holden struggles with his inability to connect with other people on an adult level, while also wanting to retreat into his own memories of childhood.

Main Characters

Holden Caulfield: The troubled, judgmental protagonist and narrator of the novel.

Phoebe Caulfield: Holden's mature ten-year-old sister, whom he loves dearly.

Stradlater: Holden's roommate at Pencey Prep, a popular, sexually active boy.

Ackley: Holden's pimply, insecure neighbor at Pencey Prep.

Jane Gallagher: One of the few girls whom Holden both respects and finds attractive.

Sally Hayes: A very attractive girl whom Holden has known and dated for a long time.

Mr. Spencer: Holden's history teacher at Pencey Prep, who unsuccessfully tries to shake Holden out of his academic apathy.

Carl Luce: A student at Columbia who was Holden's student advisor at Whooton and has a great deal of sexual experience.

Mr. Antolini: Holden's former English teacher and the adult who comes closest to reaching Holden.

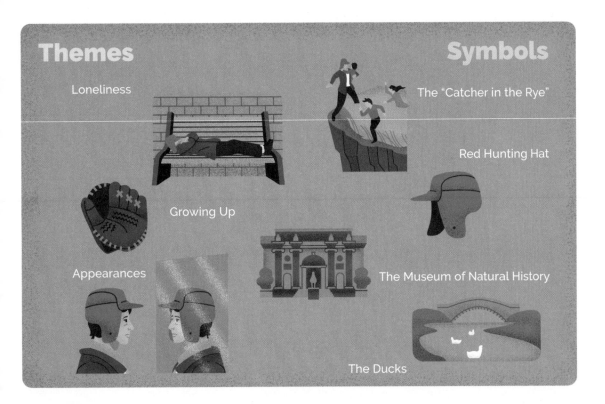

Themes

Loneliness

Growing Up

Appearances

Symbols

The "Catcher in the Rye"

Red Hunting Hat

The Museum of Natural History

The Ducks

> **B**ut what I mean is, lots of time you don't know what interests you most till you start talking about something that doesn't interest you most.
>
> *—Chapter 24*

Why does Holden hate "phonies"?

WHY ?

Holden characterizes "phonies" as people who are dishonest or fake about who they really are, or people who play a part just to fit into a society that Holden questions. Therefore, Holden hates "phonies" because they represent everything he fears or fights against, such as adulthood, conformity, and commercialism.

What Does the Ending Mean?

The Catcher in the Rye ends with Holden telling Phoebe that he is leaving home for good. When he refuses her request to take her with him, she refuses to speak to him. Knowing she will follow him, he walks to the zoo, and then takes her across the park to a carousel. He buys her a ticket and watches her ride it. It starts to rain heavily, but Holden is so happy watching his sister ride the carousel that he is close to tears. He then flashes forward to his time in some unspecified mental health facility, and mentions that he's going to a new school next fall. Holden concludes his story optimistically, but ambiguously.

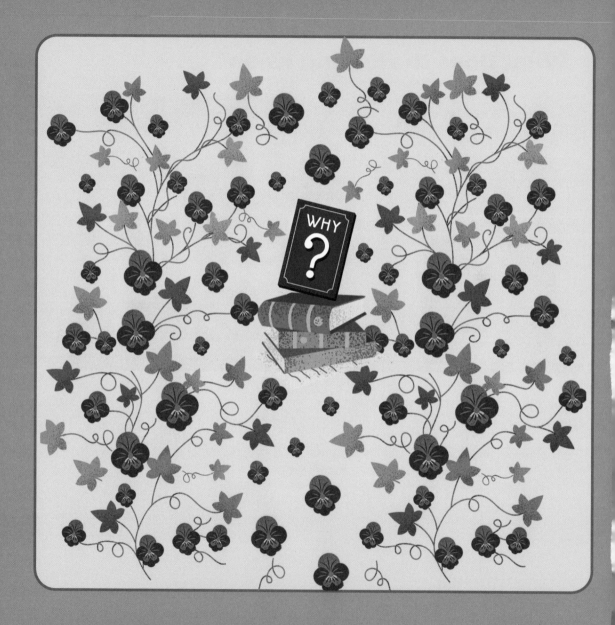